W9-AET-838

Fish

Julie Murray

Abdo
FAMILY PETS
Kids

abdopublishing.com

Published by Abdo Kids, a division of ABDO, PO Box 398166, Minneapolis, Minnesota 55439.
Copyright © 2016 by Abdo Consulting Group, Inc. International copyrights reserved in all countries.
No part of this book may be reproduced in any form without written permission from the publisher.

Printed in the United States of America, North Mankato, Minnesota.

052015

092015

 THIS BOOK CONTAINS
RECYCLED MATERIALS

Photo Credits: Glow Images, iStock, Shutterstock, Thinkstock

Production Contributors: Teddy Borth, Jennie Forsberg, Grace Hansen

Design Contributors: Candice Keimig, Dorothy Toth

Library of Congress Control Number: 2014958420

Cataloging-in-Publication Data

Murray, Julie.

 Fish / Julie Murray.

   p. cm. -- (Family pets)

ISBN 978-1-62970-901-7

Includes index.

1. Fish--Juvenile literature. 2. Pets--Juvenile literature.   I. Title.

639.34--dc23

                    2014958420

Table of Contents

Fish

Fish make great family pets.

4

Fish come in many colors.

Some are **bright**.

Some have **stripes**.

Some fish are small.

They can live in a fish bowl.

Some fish are big.

They need to live in a fish tank.

Add plants and rocks to the tank. These give the fish places to hide.

Tanks need to be kept clean.

Ellie cleans her fish tank.

Fish need food every day.

Peter feeds his fish.

Fish are fun pets to watch.

They swim all day long!

Is a fish the right pet for your family?

Fish Supplies

fish bowl

fish tank hiding spot

fish food flakes

pebbles and plants

Glossary

bright
very light and bold in color.

stripes
a long band of color that has
different colors on each side.

Index

abdokids.com

Use this code to log on to abdokids.com and access crafts, games, videos, and more!

Abdo Kids Code:
FFK9017

24